Table Of Contents

A Foreword

I thought it a good idea to put a foreword to these poems, so people can understand these words in an edifying and proper way. My purpose in this poetry is to Express. In particular, I want to express the Gift and gifts God has given me. I want to express more than the beauty and the mere feelings and emotions that are in these words and poems. I especially want to express the salvation that is in Jesus and the Holiness of God, whom is forever praised! I admit that my words are tainted because I am a sinner.   Yet I hope and pray that you could and would see the beauty in God's creation, enjoy the depths of language that God has given us, and most importantly realize how good God is. So don't look to these words as Scripture, usually they are not. Sometimes there are small phrases found in the Bible, but these poems are merely poems not Holy Scripture. Yet, do be edified by them as they remind you of the cross, the beauty of nature, the joys of healthy relationships and all the other good gifts God has given us. Always, the central focus being Jesus Christ crucified for us sinners. God gives us truth and gives our lives meaning. The depths of that meaning is found in God's love for us; revealed in death of His son on the cross. It means that Jesus is God, and God is love, and God loves us broken sinners, who deserve hell. The significance of that goes on to all Eternity. May Jesus be Praised!

Looking to the Cross

-Tyler Andrew

And I

How do I express my self inside
How do I express my self alive

Present, past, and future new
Remember the tears are falling
I'm running calm on hope that's stopped
Tender breathes of wonder warm
Filled within my fragile thoughts
Waterfalls and lilies lie
Sleeping peaceful under watchful eye
Future understood before present cared
Fately trapped in webbed mind
Crystal clear under foggy skies

And still I cry…
And still I cry…

Angelic Breath

Angelic breath, that clouded frost
Came upon the knowing self
A grace that could stop time
And fragrance of the beauty pure
Spread like fire on the wind
Delivered on the mind's front step

A human form invisible
Unearthly means that floated forth
The frost did transform to dew
And the fire never truly died

Of spirit that willed,
      A living soul
Of mind that sought
      A perfection whole

The form is larger than our minds
The spirit knew the lies of time
Eternal fire of the purest flame
That wielded strength into its name

Complete and Whole

Sleepless waters rushing within
Piecely found when the waters drain
And pouring the fears, they wash away
The Slight of sight sees …
Me, somewhere not so far away

Some potpourris fills the silence with words untold
Scents of sandalwood and cinnamon sensed within
I can slowly think about the way the sun use to taste
As you were there, to only sweeten, and bring life

As I exhaled thoughts left and stayed, both the same
Thankfulness swelled and found a home

Complete and whole

Flower

Symmetrical this symmetry of a systems end
Similar to some something simple rhymes
Written through a soul of love, a soul above
Something with that solstice touch
Focused on the simple side
The side this time it needs to fly
Complexity immensity confusion in the best of me
Already flourished past these garden walls
A f lower   of beauty in lines…   So fine
Enclosed tower of light transformed
<u>Physical lines defined?</u> The story will unwind

Purity the heavens rained
And the flower breathed the love of God

To the random thoughts

A blazing light that burns as brightly
As if combined in rayed direction

From the angels in my mind

Each wing a glint of hint that slightly
Glares a light as bright as lightning

As it thunders through a darkened sky

From the electric and our incline

Inclination raised the angels
Angles of their light divine

A blazing light of welded presence
With valleyed hills of thought to climb

From the beauty of our combine...

To my one true love, Beautiful

A wildfire of thoughts inside
All yearning for your partner's sigh
Doth sloth the time in perception's walls
A poker face, whose bluff you call

You feel when time is slowing down
Or when I am two worlds away
But remember always what we've found
Our souls are one both night and day

We need not place, nor scent, nor sound
You are with me both here and now
And I with you to joyous bring
A love, reflection on a tranquil spring

Just enough to let you know
That I could never ever let this go
Infinite as my depths inside
The ripples picture in my mind

Once forever

Once forever you will be
Lost myself, here for me
The near or far we will see
All the ugly stained on me

Life of all, forgiving grace
Sick of life, lose this race
Sometimes closer thoughts between
Always farther from within

Marching backwards, forwards true
Either or life is blue
No direction truth be seen
Endless circle, fading dream

Once forever you will be
Found myself, you with me
The need and trust I do see
All the washings I am free

Twice a Hatter

Twice a hatter pondered pausely
Found a squirrel, and fell in love
Had a child slightly scattered
Had another always smiles

Cheerful slept and joined his other
(Gracefully armed with angel wings)
Scattered cried of poison tears
Shallow bogs, and hidden fears

Two more crazies once were bore
Both of female, psychos Sighting, and Squirrelly two
Aging time as we grow tall
Fathers father, and mother's fallen

Scatted sees where light has not
Hatter's lost in wonderland
Mothers iffy, confused, and broken
Sisters finding life in ponds

Oceans grow where I have stepped
Nature's will controlled and thought
All creations in a cloud
Floating peaceful, floating soft
Never landing, always sought.

A love song…

All clear enfolded thoughts of thine
Which paint the colors in the sky
And cause the rains to fall on me
Which wash away that I might see

More than this…

And this feeling I have within
That someday soon I'll be home
Free from body, flesh and skin
Even now I'm not alone

In my heart…

In this love I cherish rest
I find a feeling star streaking high
And as I think on you as blest
That brushes magic in my eyes

Perceiving truth…

That this all was planned in holy thought
In every moment to know we were bought
By the precious blood of God
Just to say in truest Love

You are mine…

With

With strings of human kindness swelling
As each wave tenderly washes over me
And deep sought times hidden clearly just waiting
Always waiting, and always hoping for better
And so I perceive this all pervading light that all surrounds me

With this fire in my chest

As I wander through a darkened land

Staying up that last dew drop aching moment

Just to hold onto the moment of her beauty one more instant

The melancholy slowness of that joy, that passion

These are just slides of experiences

Love in its true form lives inside of us

All my heart cries out…

As fine dew mists in a morning cloud
As thought and memories circle round
As sun so softly beats us down
    All my heart cries out

As softly says the little things
As muses pondered in these strings
As gentle breezes always sing
    All my heart cries out

As creatures in their only song
As light is true and ever strong
As most and only in this throng
    All my heart cries out

    All my heart…

    All my heart…

    All my heart…   …cries to you

Burning Orbs

Succinct direct as images form
Rayed and given for now from a point
Equally dispersed as all fine lines form formless
This image illustrated as all burning glowing fiery orbs of heaven
Both waves and particles combustion expansion
Vibrations given from eternity
Words mainly waved yet Spirit
Burning serving forms of life

Capitulate

Beat beat in my heart
Thump de thump one last note
And as we see past... this world's light
... one more night

As free as free can be
Feeling more and more
So intense as these feelings fall all around me encircles
In circles and a healing recovery and something new
Capitulate my everything to the one who died for me

Clearly

Clearly as clean and succinct as words, ideals, and thought
Form and expedite in journey from one to an other
These invisible cords, these transparent realities, these clear clarities
Defining definition as these words live each its own
Stacked placed and bent as true meaning reveals…
Not from logic rational theories or necessary intelligence
Yet understanding as a gift prevails from One God
Giving each there portion of inspiration, perception, and wisdom
All encompassing love that gives to those who ask
All compassionate love that humbled Himself for His own
All truly human as He laid down His life
One thought prevails as the tree dries and the sap hinders
One thought when all seems lost and darkness broadens
One thought as the love of most grows cold

"I am with you" -- Jesus

Empty

Still enveloping
As the winter's wasted wind
Blows as softly says
 "little hope of ever life"
Of this tundra ever known
Seems still and empty there
A simple flower... withered
Fragile petals dusted thin
Hopeless the darkness
Of a world's emptiness

Given once a simple sacred word
...And the flower bloomed

Exuberant Breath

Beauty still remembering as these lines read
Aged and old across your face
Beatitudes as an answer to your age
Your hands tell more than you have said
Breathily a living air exuberant
Breathily barely long enough
As this onto you may be made clean
Borne and born again
Natural a moment but only once
To escape this God made natural prison
And shine like all glory made starry skies above
This body was born unto decay
Yet I sense a freeing
A simple sense of being

One last breath

To finally breathe forever

Eyes

Simple exquisite eyes
Gazing eyes of Lazarus
Solid piercing gentle gazing eyes
Light shedding brilliant soul gazing eyes
Simple gazing eyes…

Heartfelt

Heartfelt art felt expression

Right beside me as I dream

Waking a remembering
Seeing into the depths of self
Right inside me as I dream
And in the heart of hearts
A flame perpetual

Sourced in eternity
Sourced from above
Seen brightly shining, as holy from the heavens!
Brightly shining lighting sighing
As the song rings out,
"Searching out the depths of God"

HOLY!! HOLY!! HOLY!!

As the angels sing
A joy so intense
A voice like the rivers
Encompassing a multitude
Brazen a radiant form
As the song rings out
"Searching out the depths of God"

HOLY!! HOLY!! HOLY!!

Seen brightly shining as holy from the heavens!
As the radiant glowing transcending perfection of God shines out
And as the heavens shake and the earth goes asunder
Then we go to our heavenly home
Where God dwells forever
Then we go to our heavenly home
Where God is with us forever
As the song rings out
"Searching out the depths of God"

HOLY!! HOLY!! HOLY!!

Heatbuilt Heartbeat

This moment as it passes, like you, yes you dear
And all this spiraling contentment
Felt and Embraced

Shattering paines that are my crystallized thoughts breaking down
That are but frozen memories
In shattered pieces

And as this moment passes
In spent time all over again

An internal heatbuild heartbeat beat beat beating

Each piece of my memoir dashed
When brought close   within
Once again finds fluidity and breathes life
Once again finds feeling fondly

Liquid

A solid state of joy

A melting spring flowing from within
A heat sparking as I throw these thoughts down
A heart speaking as I listen close

It speaks one word, one word, one word

Quiet and profound, eternal and sure, pure and holy

God's word

Honey for the soul

Decadent an expression of the infinite
Invited sands of God
Summons from all eternity
Called as lights in a dark world
United integrated and graphed
To the One whom makes me clean

Decadent an expression of the infinite
Decades come and spent
Grass merely a handbreadth
Wasting away
Grass merely a handbreadth
Wasting away

These temples measured time
Encapsulate an eternity
Dwelling right inside
All seeing past and future honesty

Honey for the soul

Jesus

Knowing that all I ever need is right before me

I look yonder into the heavens

And seeing all the smallness of myself
And that all this was made from nothing, and that God did this

How can I do anything but marvel

How much more the fact that Truth came down to hold my hand
That Love itself came down to suffer for me… suffer even to the point of death
To share His joy, His rest, His life with me

And I deserve the opposite
And what can I offer Love but my praises and my pleas
To hold me tight
That I might gain the crown of life
That I might suffer for Him

All I know is that He loves me and
All I know is that I need Him

Now and forever, life or death, suffering or joy

-Jesus be my all in all-

Look Heavenward

Memories that fade or stay in momentous moments
As we the clay both described and decay

And all starry strung climbs above

Focal points of immense gravity unique memoirs of transcendent thought
Pushed and molded and formed
These rememberings transparent
And under the right light seen
Both brought beyond this infinite wall
With dimensions overlapped overlaid

Heaven beyond all, all we could imagine
And the deeper things stringent in slow and momentous movements
Pulsing as blood and life coursing through this living structure
Meaning nothing without the source

All starry heavens host above
Twinkle twinkle singing praises
To the God we love
Even then we are but created yet something more there is intended
Even though we were bound to death
Life itself humbled lowly
Spoke and molded us the meager lifeless clay

Died and rose again to impart in us all holy share divinity
That we may be all above these starry strung climbs above
Even all creation praises gently "Look how God has made us!"
And all groaning slowly waiting for our freedom
Waiting for the Son to free us
Waiting the Son to come

Love as Love

To kiss with lover's lips and soft embrace of embers true
Temper made of folded still of one's embanked of precious jewel
Your eyes they are the stars above and simple in your folded hands

Oh sweet embrace!!

Our love enhanced both through our eyes and through our hands
We dance the dance of life in true our spirits one
A simple rule to love as love in truth would do

Love Song

This is a love song
Slowly encompassing as it sings
Simply expressing subtle tender motioned insides cry
Of beauty and energy intertwined synergy
Expression past a point of view   -fragile as it walks-
Vibrant as all flowers fade
This is a love song
Caressing casting expressing character
This eternal bead
Bedded in simple thoughts
Given, the one whom never had to die
The seed planted brutally serene
This is a love song
As all lovers sing

To the giver given risen and glorified

Lovers' Eyes

Depths within lovers' eyes
A place where we would rather dwell
Where outside this death toll world fails
And roars this war so eminent
Yet temporary
And deep within these lovers' eyes
A knowledge satisfying a soul alive
A world craving our downfall
Lasting are these thoughts
As eternal as a moment continued
Taxing as the droughts…
Are these sins
Yet within those exquisite solid gazing eyes
A comfort that dwells within
A hope existing
Coaxing a gentle wave, washing over

Within these lovers' eyes

Lovers

With this kiss and so expressed
A motion of kindness inward caress
That touches deep hand to hand
And as we see our expression manifest
A look a sense so much more than this

Beyond, inside, and all around
Is this love heart thumped encompassing
Threaded care of fabric bare
And as we climb and descend on emotion's singing soliloquy
So much does all this mean to me
Like stars drop and comets stop
All I feel is our heart throb
And as time slows and tempos rise
So too do I see this in your eyes

Perpetual

Intertwined a love perpetual
Chained and bound to the one
Who is more than mentionable
The man God who says come to my table
The God who gave His only Son
Out of love for a creation that grieves His heart
Yet in the one in whom He delights
Even the one who played His part
Onto death He came fleshy
And died a traitor's death
And underneath this session
God's will shining forth
And once again I state:

In all, through all, and above all

Play and Love

Voluptuous as a stare across the room
Every single curve, every bend of light
As I watch you pass by, and as I fly
Seconds tick by, slowly and fade
Invisible this time, and you don't see me
And all I'm thinking, all my struggle in a simple word of hi, high
I land in someplace that feels like hope or home
And all I want is to play and love

Poetry's Potential Possibilities   - this is how I write -

Clearly floating in a thought

All intention sorting past
Future keenly sifting forth

Inkling written penship
Letters finally formed

Meanings twice
Form-only once

Poetry symmetry potential possibility
Progression past a single point
Pointing through a pastoral line

Perception pushed and molded
As these lines read
Yet continuing continuity
In unique ambiguity
Yet holding to its fluidity
As poetry is formed!

Rain and Fire

Rain as it falls
Luke warm tears of heaven
Rainbow colors of a smiling God
Simple playing in the waters of a dream
Pragmatic symbols of an eternity

Fire as it burns
Immense white fire of heaven
A spirit of burning passion
Simple cleansing purifying heat
Perpetual ideals of eternity

To write a poem and so expressed
This love I know in truest rest
Of place of high and holy sought
Of form indeed and fire's breath
Innately known inside my breast
A place to be a perfect nest

One love
God is love

Rain – *A Watering* –

Rain as minute idiom iota
These ideas falling into me
Seeping and maturing

This plant within
Growing and giving fruit
Both the rain and this plant
These small beginnings
Given the chance   Bloom
And given love as grace
Petals fall and fade
Dying becoming more
Coming down to be planted
The single multiplied
As this plant grows
This watering of my mind
This kingdom in my heart
This mortal coil temporary

Something deep inside
Cries for a returning
Hopes for an eternity
And loves Love

Seeming Seamless

Seeming seamless sunlit sunshine
Peering, piercing through the atmosphere
In grand morose exquisite ways
Slowly rising to its apex
Slowly with wanting to always stay

With great internal insight
Oh illuminate these times of gray
And on eternal foundations
Slowly will the lover say

I am free!! I am free!!
Christ freed me to be His Today!!

Simple, Bare, and Felt

Something simple, threaded, and bare
Just us in the hills and valleys of our thoughts
Essential movements touching in subtle tender ways
Each fingertip spreading warmth in rayed direction
Deeply contained and felt so felt
Each thought given and pondered
Each word made strong in this short and fleeting lasting moment
Rolling ecstasies in playful touch
Building and releasing all to make you feel cared for important and healthy
Sustained on a breath, breathing, breathing

-Things to wonderful for me to know-

Since

These thoughts, so thought, so true
As truly truth warms and smooths
Over all this wet clay
Molded and sculpted
Tempered and forged
Resounding instruments
Lowly now, but lifted up
Sifted and keen, lifted and clean
Something I've been since I've found you

Single Hope

A single hope hoping
As tender and fragile
Yet
Resilient a remaining
Structured and made this way
Once eternal clay
Molded, shaped, and carved
And yet it dies
And on that day
I'll shine
And never pine
As fine
To those whose kind
Eyes see light

Sparks

Friends on this hope floating island
I cry as I yearn for smiles
And something better as deep within
I see the heavens open and pour
Thousands of blessings
Sparking and flickering as they land on my heart
And in part and in whole
Heal my life and heal my soul
Just a glimpse of what is to come
All this passion heats my core

Stars

Thou sands that fills the sky
Open and vulnerable seeing through the shell
And into the deep of light and dark
We see appearing endless
Endless seas on this flat world
Soaring higher than the birds
Life not existing outside of life
Astonishing the grandeur of meek creation
Image of the creator, instruments to be played
Not being able to do anything outside of
All lights hung in huge whirling place of balance
Strung tight their chords
And as the chorus songs
Sing out and along
Both in our hearts and with a throng

Thou sands of eternal births

We are those seeming bright

Namely the stars

Superlative

Superlative this expounding
Explaining true lines trust and trying
Searching out through redemption's
Untwisted unwavering undergrowth
A source of cleansing streams
As the light dims and darkness creeps
Smothering a thickness
Flees as the true shining shines and brights
Its o u t standing
Miraculous
Both inconstant time
And frail space
And these dreams within their place
Sound light vibrations and motions stride
Reflecting absorbing refracting mine
Thoughts so small within in this time
Unwavering unimaginable inconceivable
The things God has in store for us

Turning our backs to this false fallen fake and forsaken world

And turning to the precious prestigious praying pearl, that is Christ.

Tears and Joy

Lovely is what I think
Of simple landscapes
Of fragrant flowers
And the curves of each bend in subtle daylight

Expressive is what I think
Of vibrant sunsets
Of poetic nothings
And creations fragile form groaning for its freeing

Beautiful is the thought I think
On what God has done
Both in this creation and in His character
That the God enthroned in Heaven
Would humble Himself take on weak flesh and brutally die

Beautiful wonderful magnificent awe-inspiring and Glorious

Some simple words that are spoken best with tears and joy

Tender This Moment

Tender this moment
As all fine lines read
As lovers gently touch
As soft enrapture of momentum

This moment tendered
Touched and experienced
Read thought and examined

And realized in simple words
Heard inside
Before the storm
Sheltered in a space of prayer

Kissing a remembering

Each thought precious
As they pass
And knowing this dream like state
Will one day be but a fading remembrance

When we the meek lowly and unworthy
As we shelter in a space of prayer
Lifting our heads to the coming…

The coming of the Glory

This thought so beyond our capacity

The coming of the Glory

Tender

Soft enrapture of a delicate sense of being
Fragile thoughts webbed and crystallized
These silk sheets that are memory
Hung and folded with malleable fingers

Thought given as subtle rains
Growth inside as gardens grow
Each bud to blossom each forth in love
As petals fall over naked skin

Dusted wings of flying smalls
Each one to a given flower
And then again in instinctive patterns
A balance faint yet resounding

Responding quietly

To the one

Who gives them flight

Time

In this lasting fading fleeting moment
Trying just to break the bonds
Of time and space and gravity
And all those things of temporal means
As this moment slides
Oh in-constant time, which slows just enough to watch it by
In romantic words   "to wish the moment to stay"
Grasping it and drawing it out

      Yet despite its constant change of pace
      Onward yet it marches
      And as the moment fades in a constant stream of moments
      So another comes in its own morose exquisite ways
      And in its own rhyme and rate

So hang on and let go
And tread through moments come and moments gave
Until that Day
Oh lasting Day
When our hearts all filled with joy
And as they swell and over flow
In the light of Jesus' face

Then an eternal day will shine and the moment stay
In the light of our Savior's face

Forever

With our hearts embraced by Grace

Union

Resonating intuitive frequencies frequently as all this spins
And walking straight lines through this pencil's pointing
So fine these lines which define and refine the aspect of your shape
And the beauty in your eyes sighs in retrospect as Love takes hold
Beholden as simple truths
Wash and cover you in sweet smelling spring showers
As sacred said, some simple words, reverb in ties of truth
Two souls' communion conversing completely, one word
One truth and the expanse, magnitude, definition, and depth
Unimaginable, beyond all dreams description
Saved cherished and perfect, just waiting for the day

Union to the one who makes you whole

Weather

An understanding remote
An island perpetual
These thoughts thoughtfully thought
And float on so many breezes
Which form and shift and form again
God parting my clouds

Shining

And sometimes my storms, which strike immense lights from heaven
And form glass in the soil of my mind
Or occasionally a single white lofty cloud pours in exacting location
And with the rays of paradise form
Colored bending beams
As an answer to some simple prayers… which streak across the sky
This gift immense as His gifts are

A reminder…

A whisper

A taste of   what is to come

Yes, I am His

Be longing is what I am to you
And far searching am I in this blue

All future sought and ever new
And bright and shining truth

That sources from within
With each and every note
Letting my insides know
That it's more than ok to begin

And seeing through all clear intended thought
In my heart I know wholly that I am bought
With the price of holy blood from the fount
Of eternal springs with which it brings a new life again

And all I can say is yes and amen, and that yes indeed I am His

A Gift

Supplemental these words ring
Sound out and about
Seeing through these false clouds
As storms gather round
Sounding out in arrayed majesty
Each spark plasmatic energy
Who's voice travels in recoil
As man's dreams may spoil
If not directed and troubled to keep
Prospered and treated and in secret which speaks
Those sparks intuitive inspiration
Striking where the striker strikes
Gifts from above and abode in canticles
Which sing unretractable irretraceable

In simple moments such as these

Succulent the growth entreated
Which grown from the branch
Branches to and fro tended
Intended and produce produced...

...these fruits tender yet satisfying the burden light
Conveying thought through beams of bright yet caring might
To both build and destroy these ideas given and explained
In sacred yet familiar logistics which convey the true meaning
Meaning mainly this that inspiration is given
In bright flashes of intuitive rapture
Which speaks as the giver giving from way on high as thoughts form from
Particle and waves each exclaimed as the Son shines down.   This is a gift.

Aided Renewed Dew

Aided serene peaceful and clean

All sought found and taught

Lessons learned and things made pure

In seasons such as these tones made clean

Through life and death peace and storm

Flowers bloom delicate yet exclaiming fragility and beauty

Neither toiled nor spinned yet Solomon wasn't found as glorious as these

Even as they fade resounding the grave

We have a better hope

Christ alone Heaven our home

And these bodies remade in ways we could never have asked for

Aided serene peaceful and clean

The renewed of dew of youth, our bodies are free

Born Lowly - O King

A thought as still as summer rain
And a moment as cared for, as I care for you
In time stopped and thoughts run free
In a precious space, that's only you and me
In a growing act of love enhanced
By both this seed and the heaven's rain renewed
And only knowing that these temporal things try and long to make me blue
In a world that hates and claims; bruised, beaten, and maimed
Still I long to follow the one who lead the way
Knowing it's my life and death
And causes stronger then my own
Bring me through it all, just to gain the crown of life
And it's all that matters, you oh yes, you Jesus
You are all that matters or will ever matter

Beyond all things, yet contained in flesh
Born lowly, lived fully, and died slowly

All to set us free

Broken

Broken and hopeless sitting in rags yearning for light
Captured and chained looking for right
Emptied and poor looking for sight

Needing a love loving you
Need a place secure and sure
A hand to hold

So make the statement bold and run to the place you belong
Stand against with love and overwhelm the throng
Broken and bleeding yet still hearing the song

Needing a love loving you
Need a place secure and sure
A hand to hold

It's time to go home

He Rose

Someone who cares
And as caring doth quall all of the redder intensities
So too does this passion which burns with immensity claiming
Claiming and defining classing character
Growth, is it not enough to mirror the plant who seeded you?
Both in flesh and blood and even more our spirit
Children of Thee Almighty
Children is our calling believing trusting
The words we are told, exploring the world we are born into
Merely simply cause of lack of sight doesn't make it go away
So too the hidden light of the glory burning and sensed
Another kingdom unseen but spoken of and if you are reading this
Believe if not merely on the words He spoke
Believe on the testimonies of those who witnessed and died for their testimony
Because people don't die for lack of reasons
We are awaiting a better life
A truer rest, the rest that belongs to God alone
A peace so serene
Even as the rose is beautiful so too does it know the taste of pain
It's more than worth it
These temporary trials
He is coming soon

He rose

Heart of Love

Silhouetting sunsets and requesting sunrise
On this ocean's surreal Sunkist seascape

Seeing through sunlit cascading prolific colors

A mind expanding
A heart of love
A vision true

A wandering through
A way to make it home, a path that rivets you
A straight and narrow aimed like a fruitful arrow

And this ocean if you can see it, if you can hear it and sense its salty spray
These colors vibrant caustic and intense
This sight seeing past
This mind reaching heights

With a heart of love

Sensed and felt, simple and bare, eager and hopeful, surrounded in rhyme
With originality and internality and everything as I started based in crime
Yet with no hope but hope in the love from you
Washed and clean, feeling serene
Knowing I'm nothing but ugly before you called my name

Pouring on me the waters of life
Knowing its saving powers come from Jesus taking my strife

And everything, my life, this love
Comes from you being willing, oh you sent from above

These colors caustic, cascading, and pure
These thoughts slow, profound, and enduring
And one more thought to give to you

Love like the Son, and shine like the stars, live forever, and die for your friends

With a heart of love

HYMN – Consolidated –

Oh my savior as thee words flow
Over me and in my heart they soar
Far above the lowly ground
And through the skies proclaiming
Freedom in its truest form
Jesus free us through your word
Trusting firmly in our Father
Who has spoken out creation
And created things like wisdom
In her gentle praising ways
Thoughts toward heaven are her praises
And every dream I surrender
To the one who formed me
In the secret abode He renders
Souls and bodies as He tenders
Us with strings of firm affection
As we stand on Him our rock
All proclaiming Jesus HOLY
Worshipping Him and only
Knowing peace and gently singing
Praises to the one who saved us
Even as we await His coming
Still the race we continue running
Toward our cross we humbly bear
Knowing it's the road to Heaven
Even though now here we suffer
Even when it's mixed with joy
Someday soon our Lord will call us
And all sorrow tears and heartache
Like a fading dream will leave us
In a land of purest pleasure
Where we'll worship God almighty
Singing to his HOLY name
And our bodies in their raising
Shining brighter than the stars above
Glorified strong and praising
In our Father's house we'll live
Life eternal in His Love

Inured Simple Thoughts

Expressed inured to simple thoughts
    Of you

Entangled cured and healed in this blue
And in ideas and sonnets sung
In moments clear
You on my heart is hung

Simple is my view, and in your eyes

Our heart sighs

So let go and hang on and listen to the song

        Of peace and cool rivers flow through your mind your heart
        Of sense refresh and ever shining light lighting up the night

So let go and hang on and come clean and go home

Seconds Away

Seconds away from knowing better...

All of this

And as stars streak across this blue black faded sky
I reach an answer that flares in immense white solitude
And speaking in prophetic nuances which change as easily...
As light through the clouds
Yet knowing that this was meant as every sunset is painted Brilliant
Like all fire ablaze in your eyes
Inner flames flaming sighs
As this love takes hold

Blazing meteors through the heavens that are my thoughts

Expounding of Songs

Are there words to express this song so sung so loved so held
An immense comfort being little and lowly and looking up upon my Father
An overwhelming flood of tears and hope surround
And I'm filled with an unimaginable joy and hope and love
And all need is to be less and held and sung over
And in my heart this song beyond songs
In my heart the one who made me and how and why make so much sense
And I'm great-full overwhelmingly great-full
One lasting day I can't wait but I'll wait and watch and hope and believe
Cause I hear your voice oh God above
And I need you like the plants the day
I need you like body the blood and lungs the air
And I'm unworthy and yet
You love me anyways
Who are we that you care for us
And I'm yours keep me yours

Oh God my Father Jesus

Circled Colored Spiraled and Pure -This Tendered Fabric-

One thought transcending tracing beyond erasing and mending
This fabric of weaved thought torn and tended through hands of expression
And in eyes an impression of toiled labor and cared for care caressing

As work is done

A process in action and complete in rays of thoughts escaping in contemption and
Claimed again in a simple act of control and focus as this tangent returns again to the
One who gave it freedom and returning a work spiraled and circled colored and pure
This thought this space this time this meter this sound this rhyme
Colored and circled spiraled and pure

As rest takes hold

A mended thought blessed renewed and healed from its draught and found tendered
Cared and sought in eyes of purest love and arms held just as strong
With motions sent from above a never ending son with rays as bright as the brightest
Chord and someday soon I will be there healed cared for and more

- In Jesus' Arms -

Rain

The weather is soaring

It is already pouring

On top of my eye lids

All over my skin

Simple Said Word

Consciousness awareness all inspiring essential form
Jetted and colored inception of old
Expanding and resounding seeking freedom
Finding and mending and now going home

Like butterflies which flutter in flight
Float and glide on moments and height
Seeking and looking surviving the fight
Existing as thought defending through night   -as always protecting the right-

Simple and commanded those light beings sought
Armed in a righteous and caring yet devouring sword
Chains broken and freed as a lesson is taught
The victim now unbound after the simple said word

Space of Prayer

Sheltered in a space of prayer
And deep within and overwhelmed
We see kind eyes see light
As fine lines feel forward toward and more
So too do fine eyes realize and encompass
This horizon encircled expand beyond into thought's land
So too do bounties fill and overflow when held close by our Maker's hand
This sigh of times stress and mine

How to express this thought of time and earth
And heaven and sea and lowly me
That this was all made out of nothing beyond comprehension
Yet it makes so much sense
All I want is eternity with Jesus, God with us

Together

Far beyond and in-between all conscious in an air of synergy
One two thousand years ago in my mind and in my heart
Seconds tick by seeming though that they are shy
And in the sea and in my dreams all clear and clean

Lovers' enrapture of simple thoughts
Shared by both sensations sought
That you too may see this true
That true love and sex in a loving coo

Is not skewed when your heart speaks of love
And that in the right light shines as bright
One in body, heart, and mind
That this too is worship of a kind

When brought together under God's arms of love
Simply seen and given be unto this too be made clean
And sung under eyes bright with love and sight
To live as one and share a life till we are called home to the truer shining Son

Home Again

Separate and then come again; Always farther from the night; Can you see this
light; Shining shining bright; Hear the call eclisiasticus; Answer with the heart,
known deep known deep; i cry i smile; I'm home again.

-Tyler Andrew

God My Love

God forever dwelt in Glory
Up to you this heart song sings
As with loving kindness guide me
Drench my soul this morning dawning
With your sweet reviving dew
And in all times ever coming
Loud professing of my love
That you my God gave to me
By your Son's out pouring blood
And forever are my praises
For the Good you've done for me

God my Love I am Thy creature
God my Love I profess Thee

Bridge

(Each word made perfect in cascading felt and pounding droplets washing
over as each word makes full with the breadth of meaning. The deeper
qualities right beneath the surface feeling and breathing though under water.
Each one given life in momentous movements in an innocence of trust which
speaks to the softer side if one would but listen to their story of life and love
and all that is beyond, this idea of thought understanding and connection.
That I do indeed hear your voice and follow you who spoke love into my heart,
with all these words that build and voice in climax and release each wave
conveying thought each thought made true, and if you can hear this then I've
bridged across to you)

An Offering a Plea

My life an offering to the one I Love
An offering to Love itself named in the sacred place
Oh Jesus come soon and hear, look down and see
Just lowly me striving to be free
My life an offering to you Jesus
All insides vital come soon Lord
These whispers of need these grasped thoughts these pleas
Oh please Jesus come soon

A Prayer of Thanks

All expressing are my insides
Desires burning love for thee
You Lord Jesus are my savior
Blessing me my soul with you
Putting your most Holy name
On my heart and mind and calling
Me to life with you on high
I will ever be yours praising
How deep and wondrous is your love
Grace me Lord with your presence
And take me home with you above

Wash me clean with thy pure blood
Fill me: body, mind, and soul with pure gifts
And forever your hand lead me
Guide me always with your love

Daylight's Dawning

From the darkest night this daylight's dawning
Embraced and sweetness is this light that's shining
Deeply strongly in my heart and in my soul
Joy intense of Love's great gifts
Love embraced embracing me
Light's strong sword and gentle whispers
With tender compassions set me free
Breaking chains
Dawning light
Heart now swelling
And Love's true sight

"God is Love"

Real Eyes   -Realize-

Realize these real eyes and see through these colors to the true

Blues greens and red and yellow hues

Inside these bright clear eyes

Inside the heart and mind and everything deep inside

Love, spirit, soul, everything that matters feeling deep and whole

Gazing far beyond the sky, the sun, the stars

Seeing beyond and eyes opened gazing though the material, a vision whole

God's love surrounding, fire and angels all ablaze

And the Lord sitting on His throne

Gazing vision in these eyes, realize, real eyes

Waters of Life

Honesty indwelling hearts that need be with love's deep pool

The smallest taste of loves true drink

A single drop let on your heart

The coolest taste of sweeter sweet all fires out of hell's fierce fire

Those flames are quenched and fresh water pours

Truth sincerity trust love and more

A Thought A Cross

If you can hear and see this thought
Where precious prayers and hopes are brought

    Of caring hands and caring eyes
    Of everything that's true inside

I'll say to you my friend my deer
With love in truth and without fear
That beauty fails and flowers fall
Yet love remains to hold us all

    In caring hands through caring eyes
    In purest truth that is inside

I hope in hope you understand
That through His blood with nails in hands
That God alone can keep us true
To mend our lives and make us new

    With caring hands and caring eyes
    With love of truth that is inside

To send this thought across to you
I hope you like it as I do

    A thought A cross

    <B

Butterflies

Butterflies throw colors

Dusted wings of memory

Reverb through the air

Beauty Seen

Beauty seen and Beauty be
All confessed and made clean
Truth in hands of folded care
Subtle moments of precious prayers

And just a thought
A single seed
A moment caught
Seen in the air

A butterfly in time step slowed
Threw colors vibrant pure and bold
With dusted wings of memory seen
Through reverb motions these words sing

Expressed a core and hope renewed
Expressed a soul hopefull
And true

Flowers

All flowers strewn in vast array
In colors bright, all petals dewed
Reaching upward through the day
Healing growing in their ways

The flowers bloomed, the flowers young
Happy were they as they sung

Shifting dancing in the sun

Two Flowers

Two Flowers entwined in love
With supple thoughts come flowing from
The sweetest scents they found and saved
To remember us this precious day

Fresh Fallen Snow

Fresh fallen snow in purity
I hope to thee to whiter be

O Lord my God
O Jesus please

Cleanse me and hear my plea

For all I have to you I give
Far on high Lord there you reign
The highest heights above all things

And in your hands

A broken me

Who wants and begs to be clean

Whiter than fresh fallen snow